Yes & Amen
A PRAYER COLLECTION

R. DeAndre Johnson
with art by Ibraim Nascimento

Art by Ibraim Nascimento
Book Design by Kelsey Johnson

ISBN: 979-8-8515-8024-6
Imprint: Independently published

Yes & Amen
A PRAYER COLLECTION

"Prayer is not primarily about words, it's about posture. The words, punctuation, similes, and metaphors we engage are creatures of the postures of our soul. In this remarkable and vulnerable collection, we experience the author as worshiper, questioner, pastor, lamb, and much more. A soul that refuses to hide. The gentle and fierce creatures of Johnson's prayer-postures come alive, aided by Nascimento's imaginative and evocative art. Deep calls to deep as these prayers and images invite, beguile, and entice the reader's soul. A bridge of recognition unfurls and we cannot but... pray."

—Jorge Lockward, *artist, musician, theologian*

"Ever since I've known Rev. DeAndre Johnson, his way of being the world has been one of abiding joy, holy patience, exquisite attention to others, and deep soulful connection with creation. The carefully crafted words of this collaborative prayer book will show you only a glimpse of the deep wells of his faith and concern for justice. Read it, use it as a resource for leading worship or personal devotion, or share with a friend. This offering will serve as a blessing poured out upon the reader to repeatedly behold and as words to cling to when life renders us speechless."

—Katie McKay Simpson, *pastor, author, teacher*

"DeAndre allows us to eavesdrop on his very intimate and holy conversations with God. His connection with the Holy has produced beautiful, deep, yet simple prayers and praises that say what many are thinking but can't quite find the words. This book offers each of us an opportunity to experience communicating with God in new ways, while opening us up to unimaginable possibilities. DeAndre makes it possible for you and me to feel the same strong reassuring connection to God that he does by drawing us in so very close to a loving, generous God of every time, including beginnings, endings, and in between. Thank you, my friend, for constructing prayers that give us a confidence that God hears us."

—Leo Tyler, *pastor, coach, author*

"These prayers give voice to the soul's deepest longings. They reverberate with sounds of peace and love and joy. They are inclusive and tender. Pray them and you will be blessed."

—Bishop Janice Riggle Huie

"As I read DeAndre's prayers, I am ushered into the holy. DeAndre's words and Ibraim's illustrations are a sacred combination that ought to guide every reader into that thin space where heaven and earth come so close they almost touch. While written at specific time in our lives, they have a way of transcending time, space, and place. These prayers should be prayed and prayed and prayed again."

—Bishop Cynthia Fierro Harvey

"Throughout the COVID-19 pandemic, many of us searched for words of hope that expressed our shared experience honestly. In this season, I turned daily to the powerful prayers offered by The Reverend DeAndre Johnson. These prayers, coupled with the illuminating art of Ibraim Nascimento, were a regular gift of gratitude and grace. DeAndre's extraordinary ability to bless others through prayer gave voice to the deepest longing of our hearts during that challenging and complex season. I am so glad we now have these prayers in a single volume, for they continue to be a blessing. I will turn to them again and again over the course of my days."

—Joe Stobaugh, *pastor, artist, musician*

FOREWORD

When people are struggling with the concept of prayer,
I encourage them to say, "God, what I want to say to you today is...",
hoping that they will find their way into a life-giving conversation.
I thank God that for an incredible season during the global pandemic,
DeAndre Johnson devoted himself to what he wanted to say to God.
I'm so glad he invited us to listen in on that conversation.

DeAndre's command of biblical imagery and poetic sequence
take my breath away, and his vulnerability is like an oasis of truth
telling in a desert of denial. The petitions are real, the heartache is
real, and the assurance of God's love is real because DeAndre's trust in
God is real. By taking off his own mask, he invites us to do the same.

He's not afraid to ask God for help with lifting off the "weight of
indifference," and his joy in announcing the presence of God's grace
is like a drop of honey after bitter herbs. I hope these prayers will
comfort, challenge, and shape you. They gave me real hope in the
midst of a difficult season.

—John Thornburg, *poet, pastor, song-enlivener*

CONTENTS

Praise for today
Praise for wonders
Praise for grace
Praise for the normal
Praise for mirrors and windows
Praise for this season
For a more perfect praise
Praise for community

A prayer for today
A prayer for the start of a new _____
A prayer for decision making
A prayer for the how
A prayer for the angry
A prayer for us
A prayer for the caring
A prayer for the work of love
A prayer for the repentant
A prayer for answers
A prayer for the waiting
A prayer for the ready
A prayer for the settled
A prayer for the sublime and simple
A prayer for the tired
A prayer for the still mad
A prayer for the tiny seed
A prayer for the knowing
A prayer for the church
A prayer for more
A prayer for healing
A prayer for all peoples
A prayer for remembering

A prayer for truth
A prayer for innocence
A prayer for power
A prayer for listening
A prayer for words
A prayer for light
A prayer for mercy
A prayer for a good _____
A prayer for trusting again
A prayer for change
A prayer for nuance
A prayer for dislike
A prayer for escaping violence
A prayer for escaping death
A prayer for traveling
A prayer for stopping and moving again
A prayer for exodus
A prayer for better
A prayer for returning
A prayer for love
A prayer for the journey

Part 3: Promise

Today is the day
To God, the Lord
To the God of Every Time
To a Generous God
To the God of the In-Between
To the God of Communion and Community
In the Name Of
To the God Who Weeps
To a Gracious God
To a "Do Nothing" God
To the Compassionate God
To the God of Yes/No

FROM THE AUTHOR

As the world approached the close of a rather tumultuous 2020 with an almost desperate hope for new beginnings in the new year, I began to feel a deep calling to start the new year in prayer. In particular, I felt called to write and offer prayers as a kind of holy resistance against the flood of negativity and hopelessness that seemed to pervade my social media feed.

So, for almost every night since New Year's Day 2021, I spent some time reflecting on the day, writing down whatever words came to mind in response (whether prayers of confession, lament, thanksgiving, praise or adoration) and posting them on Facebook and Instagram. Somewhere along the way my good friend, the prophet-artist-priest Ibraim Nascimento, reached out, having seen some of these prayers on Facebook, and asked if he could pray with me through his own art — for which I have been very grateful. Through his incredible artistry, Ibraim's own faith and passion for connecting others deeply to the gift of *imago dei* within has helped these prayers become healing balm for some and a surprise of grace for many — including myself.

—R. DeAndre Johnson

PART 1
Praise

Praise for today

Lord, today I am grateful.
I'm grateful for the promise of blue skies,
   the joy of impossibly round robins,
   the laughter of children,
   the patience of a preschool teacher,
   the comfort of the voice of an old friend,
   the peace of feeling at home,
   the satisfaction of a job well done,
   the pleasure of a good nap,
   the relief of renewed kinship,
   the encouragement of belonging,
   the inspiration of a good story,
   the hope of newfound friendship.
Lord, today I am grateful for all of these
   and the grace they bring.
But please, Lord, in your mercy,
help me to choose gratitude tomorrow as well,
   so that I don't miss any of your
      grace-filled surprises.

Amen

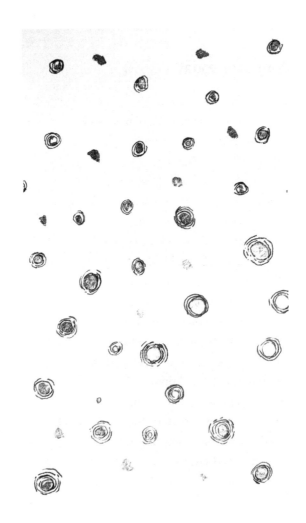

Praise for wonders

God of all things,
you fill life with
wonders too numerous to count —
   the brightness of a genuine smile,
   the warmth of a needed hug,
   the surprise of a thoughtful gift,
   the pride of a worthwhile job done right,
   the power of a kind word,
   the release of an apology,
   the relief of forgiveness,
   the expansiveness of freedom,
   the joy of families reunited,
   the hope of a new day.
Let me not miss any of these you have for me,
   whether today or in any of my tomorrows.
And by your grace,
   let me also not miss my opportunity
   to be a wonder for any of your other children.

Amen

Praise for grace

God, I want to thank you for grace,
   your unseen hand of undeserved
      blessing and favor,
      forgiveness and acceptance,
      calling and purpose.
By it I am assured over and over
   that you are with me and you are for me,
and I am summoned to vision and task.
So, teach me once more
   the humility of an unseen grace
so that I may learn
   how to bless without taking credit.
And please, in your mercy,
   show me again the extravagant beauty
      of a grace so undeserved that
   it must always be given, never taken.

Amen

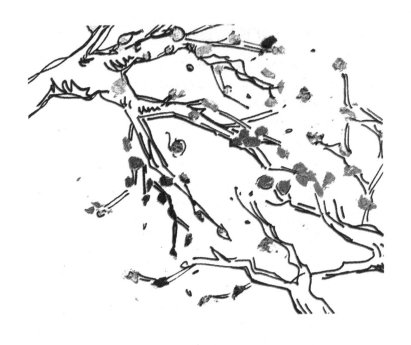

Praise for the normal

I saw that, Lord.
I saw the bright red cardinal singing away,
    and was suddenly aware of new mercies.
I saw the way they held hands,
    and was at once grateful to know love.
I saw the email between friends,
    and was moved again by compassion shared.
I saw the latest post
    and was athirst for authentic community.
I saw the news today
    and was summoned to being.

How clever of you, Lord,
    to capture my attention
        through the serendipity of normalcy.
I hope I don't make you
    work too hard in doing so.
Even still, by your grace,
    help me to never miss you,
        your calling,
            or your blessing
    in any of the randomness of my day.

Amen

Praise for mirrors and windows

God of every wonder,
thank you for giving us mirrors to see who we really are —
   so beautifully created in many hues
     yet suspicious of each other's true value,
   so creatively inventive,
     yet dismissive of talents rivaling our own,
   so incredibly gifted for love and compassion,
     yet guarded against being in community,
   so abundantly blessed and forgiven,
     yet fearful of being found guilty and empty.

Bring us again into the light, O God,
   that we may behold
     the wonder of your grace,
   transforming each wrinkle and blemish
     into a window of what we may yet become.
In the name of Him who said "Come and see."

Amen

Praise for this season

Lord, I thank you for the rain.
Though it is messy and ugly
   it nourishes and sustains the unseen life
      till it can finally burst forth
         in breathtaking beauty.
Thank you for the rain.

Lord, I thank you for the cold of winter.
Though it is unfeeling and hard to bear,
   it brings the gift of slowing down
      whereby the living can know and feel again
         the warmth of community.
Thank you for the cold.

Lord, thank you for the reminder that
   the life you give
      does not erase ugliness and discomfort
   but transforms it into a crucible for new life.
So by your grace, I'm staying put
   and I choose now to enjoy this season —
even as I eagerly await to see
   what you will do in the next.

Amen

For a more perfect praise

O God, I think I owe you an apology.
My worship has been too self-centered.
Though I've been truly grateful,
    I must confess that my "thank you"
        has really meant "More please?"
When I come before your presence,
    my praise moves too quickly
        from pure adoration to petition,
        from heartfelt devotion to requests,
        from holy reverence to overtures.
Forgive me, Lord.
By your grace deliver me from a hollow praise
    that always expects a return on investment,
and reveal to me again the absolute joy
    of tarrying in your presence,
    of marveling at your wonders,
    of beholding the beauty of your glory.
Teach me how to adore you for you —
    simply as the only wise God —
        and not for what you can do or give.
Teach me a God-centered worship,
    so that I may praise you most perfectly.
In the name of Him who taught us to pray,
    "Our Father in heaven,
        hallowed be your name."

Amen

Praise for community

Gratitude. Praise. Wonder. Adoration.
All these belong to you, O God,
for who else can make strangers into friends,
    friends into family,
        families into community —
    turning awkwardness into ballet,
        silence into laughter
            and suspicion into hope?
Thank you for the joy of friendship.
Thank you for the delight of being friended.
Thank you for the assurance of kinship.
Thank you for the peace of belonging.
Thank you for the reminders that you are here,
    and I am never alone.

Amen

PART 2
Petition

A prayer for today

Today is your day, Lord.
Not mine,
   not theirs,
     not ours,
but yours.
Help me to see each ray of sunlight,
   each drop of rain,
   each gust of wind,
as a constellation of grace,
   signs of your working in me,
     through me, and around me.
Keep my eyes open
   to see you in all the hidden places
     and hidden faces I encounter today.
Keep my mind ever marveling
   at the wondrous depth of your love
     and kindness to us.
Keep my heart malleable
   to your infinite, all-encompassing grace.
Keep my hands and feet courageous and bold,
   willing to risk the dare
     that whatever you have for me today
       is far greater than my fear.
This is your day, O Lord,
   and I am humbled again
by your merciful invitation to join you in it.
Thank you for this day.

Amen

A prayer for the start of a new _____

Eternal God, thank you for the gift of time —
   for the letting go and the sting of loss,
   for the starting over and the embrace of newness,
   for the crying out and the hunger to make it right,
   for the sorrowing and the hope for better days,
   for the dying and the assurance of death's end,
   for the living and the lives of those who yet live,
   for the trying new things
      and the surprise of creative genius,
   for the failing and the comfort of forgiveness,
   for the waiting... and the waiting...
      and the waiting... and the holiness of waiting,
Thank you for the gift of time and
   the gift of grace for every time...
and the reminder that I cannot control
   or run away from either.

Amen

A prayer for decision making

Lord, it's hard to know what to do sometimes.
There are too many decisions,
   too many opinions,
   too many risks,
   too many mistakes,
   too many lives to love and loves to live.
I don't know what do or how to be, Lord,
   but I know you. I trust you.
Give me wisdom to choose your good will for each moment.
Give me grace to live your good will in each moment.
Give me faith to believe again that no matter what I choose,
   your good will is still possible for each moment.

Amen

A prayer for the how

So Lord, how do you do it?
How do you stay true
   when everyone and everything around
      claims a different truth?
How do you love indiscriminately
   when everyone and everything around
      pronounces certain ones unloveable?
How do you believe unswervingly
   when everyone and everything around
      impugns conviction?
How do you have hope
   when everyone and everything around
      profits from the perpetuation of misery?
How, Lord? How?
Show us again through story and sign
   the wonder of your call and
   the wonder-filled power of your Holy Spirit
that summons us to and anoints us for
   purpose beyond circumstance.
And by your grace,
make all your purposes ever bold in us
   till everyone and everything around
      is astounded and stupefied into praise.

Amen

A prayer for the angry

O God of every season and every purpose,
   teach me the right use of anger.
Show me how to cry out without lashing out.
Show me how to disagree without dismissing.
Show me how to fight without violence.
Show me how to lose and still love the winner.
Teach me, O God, to have a grace-filled anger,
so that I may always know
   the difference between vengeance and justice,
     and may be ever willing to lay
       my outrage aside for the makings and workings of peace.
In the name of Him who said both "Woe to you..."
   and "Father, forgive them..."

Amen

A prayer for us

O great God of all truth and light,
    they need you;
    we need you;
    I need you —
        now...
           ...like, right now.
They/we/I need to hear your voice again,
    summoning us from death to life through death,
    bidding us to find you in the quiet of small things,
    singing over and into us a love too deep for words.
They/we/I need to feel your presence again,
    pervading our thoughts with the awe of your power,
    invading our hearts with the shock of your grace,
    restoring our lives with the release and relief of forgiveness.

They/we/I need you, O God,
    again...
      ...and again...
        ...and again...
until there is no more they/we/I,
    ...only us...
      ...only you.
    and "Father, forgive them..."

Amen

A prayer for the caring

Lord, sometimes I worry.
I worry about my children...
   are they healthy enough,
      happy enough,
         holy and whole enough?
Have I done enough to secure their place among the blessed?
But then I remember the others...
   are they healthy enough,
      happy enough,
         holy and whole enough?
Who will secure their place
   among the blessed?
      Who?

Lord, sometimes I worry —
   not whether there is enough for the need,
      but that the need outmatches
         my willingness to care.
Forgive me. Heal me.
Deliver me from the oppression of indifference
   into the delight of an uncommon compassion,
      the freedom of an unrestrained generosity,
         and the joy of an uninhibited hospitality.
In the name of the Lord who
   "is gracious and compassionate,
      slow to anger
         and rich in love."

Amen

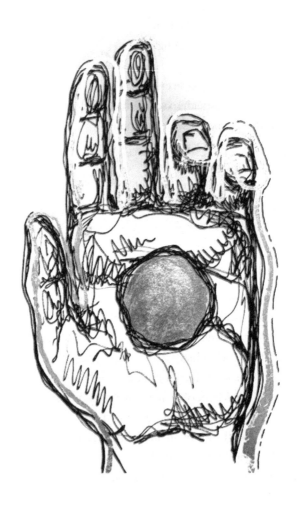

A prayer for the work of love

O gracious and ever loving God,
you so ably hold in your tender care
   both the whole company of heaven
      and an infinitude of creatures
         all dependent upon your mercy —
            but how do you do it?
How do you make your love and compassion
   so broad and wide,
      so constant and sure,
         so personal and particular?
And how do you make it flow so easily
   even when rejected, denied,
      criticized, and scorned?
However you do it, please teach me.
Help me to get past the mere wonder of love
   so that I can get to the work of love
      you desire to do in and through me.

Amen

A prayer for the repentant

God in heaven,
there is so much to say,
  so much to confess,
    so much to lament,
      so much to regret,
        so much to forgive,
  So. Much. To. Repent.
Where do I begin?
  How do I even start…
    again?
Sing to me once more the words of grace —
"Come."
  "Be."
    "See."
      "Wait."
        "Listen."
          "Remember."
            "Live."
— so that I may find my ground again,
    and my heart may echo your grace-song
  till all of my life and the world around me
    is transposed and transfigured
      into the song of redeeming love.

Amen

A prayer for answers

Lord, sometimes I just don't like your answers.

I ask "Why?" and you answer, "Will you trust?"

I ask "What?" and you answer, "Will you believe?"

I ask "When?" and you answer, "Will you wait?"

I ask "How?" and you answer, "Will you love?"

I ask "Who?" and you answer, "Will you go?"

You refuse to give me
    settled answers of easy comfort,
choosing instead to interrogate me so thoroughly that I am left
    unnerved, disturbed, haunted, antagonized,
    and ultimately whole.
Lord, I don't like your answers,
    but I need them just the same.
So, please, keep them coming.

Amen

A prayer for the waiting

How long, O Lord?

How long does it take for love to take root?

How long does it take for peace to settle?

How long does it take for justice to flow?

How long does it take for chains to break?

How long does it take

   for righteousness to reign?

How long?

Grant us patience in the waiting,

   faith in the doubting,

   and hope in the believing.

Sanctify us in grace and

   send us again in Holy Ghost power

   to be emissaries of your new creation —

and in your mercy,

keep us in unease

until we become more eager

   to work with you

     than we are for you to stop.

Amen

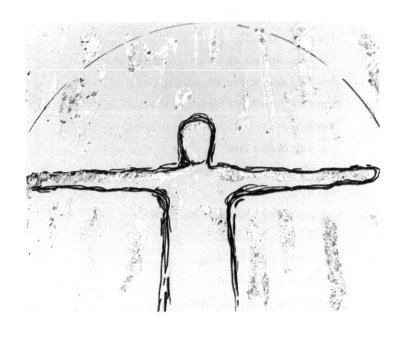

A prayer for the ready

Lord, I think I'm ready now.
I'm ready to laugh again till my belly hurts —
   but please no more crying.
I'm ready for warm hugs again —
   but please no more distancing.
I'm ready to SANG again —
   but please no more silence.
I'm ready to believe again —
   but please no more disappointments.
I'm ready to love again —
   but please no more wounds.
I'm ready to breathe again —
   but please no more death.
I think I'm ready, Lord,
   if you can accept these terms.
If not,
   then please move me,
     mold me,
   and make me serviceable to you
     till I'm ready to accept your terms.

Amen

A prayer for the settled

Lord, can we just stay here for a while?

I think I like where I am right now.

I like the feeling of safety and security here,

    so please don't ask me to move.

I like the comfort of my inner circle,

    so please don't ask me to reach out.

I like the coherence of my own reasonings,

    so please don't ask me to expand.

I like the predictability of my life here,

    so please don't ask me to follow.

Please don't call me to give or do any more,

    because that choice is too hard —

        to settle or be converted.

By your grace,

help me to discern the difference

    between easy and living,

and by your Spirit,

make me brave in answering your call,

    trusting you to mercifully lead me to better.

Amen

A prayer for the sublime and simple

O great and glorious God,
you created worlds beyond knowing
    with just a word — is that really all it takes?
You birthed a people to bless and be blessed,
    all with a single promise —
        is that really all it takes?
You healed diseases, disorders, and divisions
    with just a touch — is that really all it takes?
How sublime yet simple is your work, Lord!
Can you, please, do it again for me?
Please, speak in me that word
    that will open my world to possibilities
        yet imagined.
Please, help me to receive again the promise
    that can birth in me
        belonging and sacred purpose.
Please, heal me with a touch
    that will release me to wholeness
        and revive in me the power of mercy.
Please... so that I might know again just how
    sublime yet simple is your work in me.

Amen

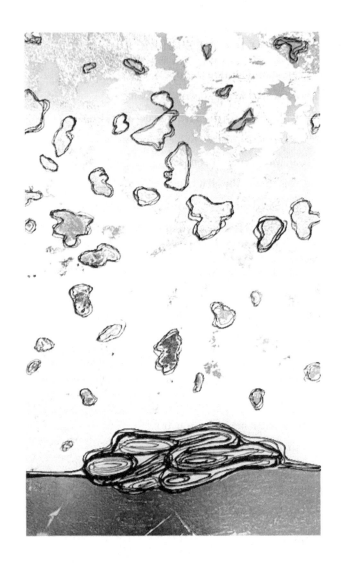

A prayer for the tired

I'm tired today, Lord.
I'm tired of feeling exhausted
  like an empty pen,
    able to make an impression
      but not quite able to make its mark.
I'm tired of feeling aimless
  like paper caught in the wind,
     always moving but never towards
     its intended purpose.
I'm tired of feeling helpless
  like a ball rolling downhill,
   needing assistance to stop
   and change directions.
I'm tired of feeling frustrated
  like an engine with no oil,
   working so hard yet gaining nothing
    but grinding resistance at every turn.
I'm tired, Lord, and I don't know how to fix it.
So, I think I'll just wait here and rest awhile
  till goodness and mercy can catch up,
and I can learn again that change will come.

Amen

A prayer for the still mad

Lord, I'm still mad,
    but I'm choosing gratitude today.
I'm still mad about a world that
    feels distressingly distressed,
but I'm grateful for cool breezes
      and sunny days.

I'm still mad about a world that
    has to define which lives matter —
      as if it should be a choice —
but I'm grateful for rising voices of pride
    and affirmation.

I'm still mad about a world filled with
　　those who peddle and prey upon
　　　　the politics of fear,
but I'm grateful for truth-seekers, truth-tellers,
　　and fact-checkers.

I'm still mad about a world where too many of
　　your children live under threat of violence,
　　　　but I'm grateful for good samaritans
　　　　　　willing to cross borders and policies.

I'm still mad about a world where too many of
　　those called by your Name
　　　　refuse the humility of correction,
but I'm grateful for mercy that
　　treats us better than we deserve
　　　　and grace that teaches us how to be better.

Lord, I'm mad but so grateful that
　　you choose to be with us in this world,
　　　　you chose to become us in this world,
　　　　　　you chose us in this world.

Now Lord, in your mercy and by your grace,
　　make both my gratitude and my anger
　　　　serviceable for your work of redemption
　　till all this world is wholly made new
　　　　by the power of your Holy Spirit.

In the Name of the One who "did not send his Son
　　into the world to condemn the world
　　　　but to save it through him."

Amen

A prayer for the tiny seed

Great God of boundless possibilities
  and matchless grace,
thank you for the wonder and mystery
    of a tiny seed.
In it you have hidden the secrets
  of your power and your kingdom —
for how is it that something so lifeless
  can produce such a magnificent tree
    whose leaves give air for breathing,
    whose fruit gives food for nourishing,
    whose bark gives medicine for healing,
    whose sap gives relief for the stinging,
    whose branches give shelter for dwelling,
  and whose life gives beauty for refreshing?
And how is that
  though you have given me this seed
    to tend and to nurture and to cultivate,
I have no power to make it grow?
Only you can, only you will.
So, by your grace,
  give me more faith in believing,
    more patience in waiting,
  and more perseverance in working,
trusting with assurance in your absolute power
    to awaken the dead
and unlock every hidden potential in all things,
  including me.

Amen

A prayer for the knowing

Lord, I know that you know everything, and I don't.
 I know that you can do anything, and I can't.
 I know that you are everywhere, and I'm not.
 I know that you love everybody, and I won't.
I do know these things,
 but I often wonder if
 my inability affects your ability
 or that your restraint might be impotence.
Tell me again the richness of your wisdom,
 show me again the constancy of your presence,
 sing over me again the depth of your love,
till all my wonderings and fears
 are once more overmatched
 by the wonders of your grace.

Amen

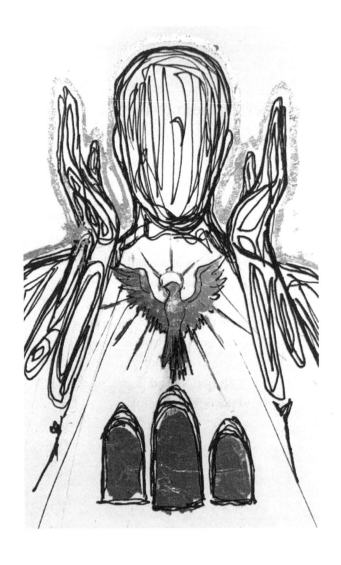

A prayer for the church

Holy Spirit, come and repossess your church.
We grew tired in waiting for you
   and have strayed too far from the places
     we first met you.
We found more efficient ways to do business
   and have gone too long without listening
     for your direction.
We placed confidence in our own experience
   and have become too oblivious
     to your work around us.
Forgive us, Lord.
In your mercy and by your power,
   rush right into our hallowed spaces
     and disrupt all our scheming,
       all our dreaming,
       all our politicization,
       all our polarization,
       all our theologies,
       all our charities —
for none of it matters without you.
Without you, none of it matters.
Come, Holy Spirit. We desperately need you.

Amen

A prayer for more

Lord, is this all there is?
Should I look for, can I expect more?
I want more, Lord —
   more joy to outlast any sorrow,
   more peace to quiet every fear,
   more hunger for righteousness to reign,
   more thirst for justice to flow like rivers of life,
   more power to set every captive free,
   more fire to share the good news,
   more hope for the potential of every tomorrow.
Give me more, O God.
Make me ready for more, O God,
   so that I may rise to the fullness
      of your image in me.

Amen

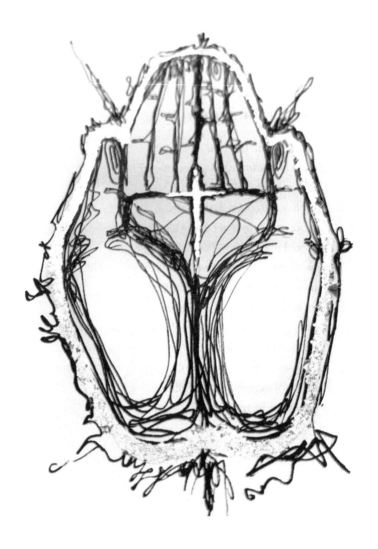

A prayer for healing

Heal us, O Lord.
Heal us of the poison of fear
   that so easily and stealthily invades
      our thinking till we become
         paralyzed by worry
      and doubtful of your goodness for us.
Speak to us again your word
   of peace and stillness,
   of calm and assurance,
      and make us whole.
Heal us of the scourge of anger
   that threatens to consume us from within
      till we lose all good sense
         of truth and righteousness and justice.
Anoint us again with the oil of gladness
   so that we might feel
      the relief and release of mercy
         and make us whole.
Heal us of the curse of pride
   that so perniciously distorts our ability
      to truly know ourselves in the light
         of who you really are.
Lay your hands on us
   and make us know once more
      the weight of your awe-some power
         till we are humbled into wholeness.
You, O Lord, are the One who said,
   "I am the LORD, who heals you."
Heal us, we pray.

Amen

A prayer for all peoples

O God of all peoples,
by your grace you have
   placed us in families and tribes,
      cultures and nations,
but we are wooed away by a separatist spirit
   into believing that we are better alone,
      that we can discover the truth alone,
      that we can be made whole alone —
   or at least, without those people.
Deliver us, Lord,
   and lead us again into
      the humble freedom of community.
And show us how to belong to each other,
   even as we belong to you.
In the name of Jesus who prayed "...that they may be one
   as we are one — I in them and you in me — so that
   they may be brought to complete unity. Then the world
   will know that you sent me and have loved them even
   as you have loved me."

Amen

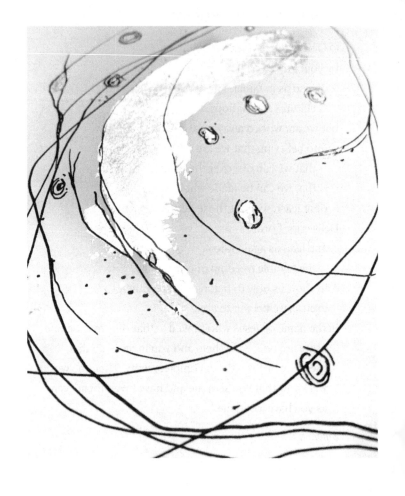

A prayer for remembering

O great God of everything glorious,
I just remembered that
   you make all things beautiful in their time.
I remember the time
   when loneliness threatened to overwhelm me
      but the timely voice of a friend lifted me to life. Thank you.

I remember the time
   when trouble surrounded me on every side
      but the timely generosity of a friend
         opened the way for peace. Thank you.

I remember the time
   when disaster stole away my sense of safety
      but the timely work of friends
         brought me to restoration. Thank you.

I remember the time
   when guilt pressured me into shame
      but the timely apology of a friend
         made real the possibility of forgiveness. Thank you.

God, I forgot that beauty takes time.
So, in all my times of distress,
   help me remember that you are working still,
      and give me faith enough
         to view all my neighbors not as suspicious
      but as promising brokers
         of your marvelous grace.

Amen

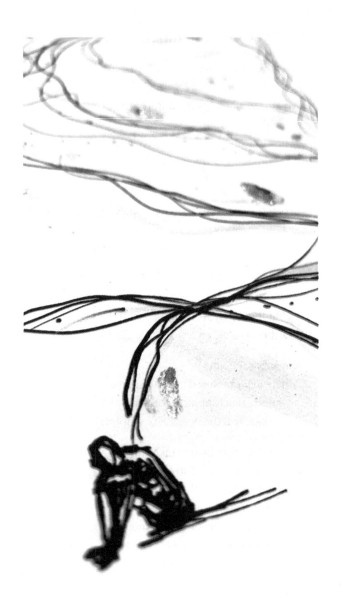

A prayer for truth

O God of all things pure and true
   and hidden and secret.
You ask "Where are you?"
   and I hide in shame.
You ask "Who told you...?"
   and I search for blame.
You ask "Is anything too hard...?"
   and I laugh in disbelief.
You ask "How long will you grieve...?"
   and I realize I must let go.
You ask "Whom shall I send...?"
   and I rise to purpose.
You ask "Will anyone rob God?"
   and I confess my complicity.
Lord, your questions continue to
   haunt and disturb my settled soul,
      ferreting out all my truth
so that I am laid bare in the light of your truth
   — and made whole.
So, please,
   keep questioning me, Lord,
      till I become only "Yes" and "Amen."

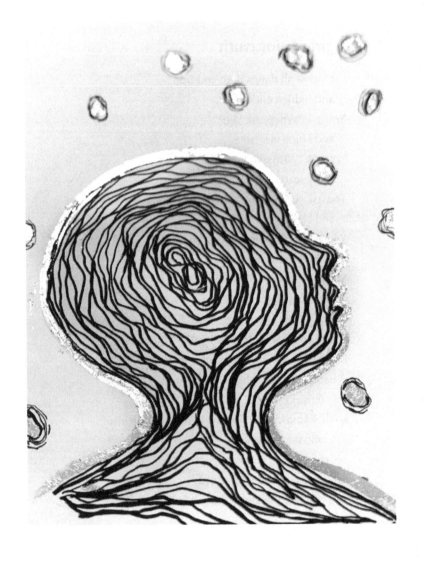

A prayer for innocence

Lord, I'm tired of being a grownup,
   please make me a kid again.
Help me to marvel again
   at the wonder of simple things
   and to appreciate the power of the small.
Show me again
   the promise of wide-eyed curiosity
   and the joy of new discovery.
Teach me the courage of innocence
   and the daring of honest questions.
Make me able again to simply
   believe what you say without suspicion —
   to only have faith that you still hold
     my life and my best interests
       in grace-filled, loving care.
In the name of Him who says,
   "Let the children come."

Amen

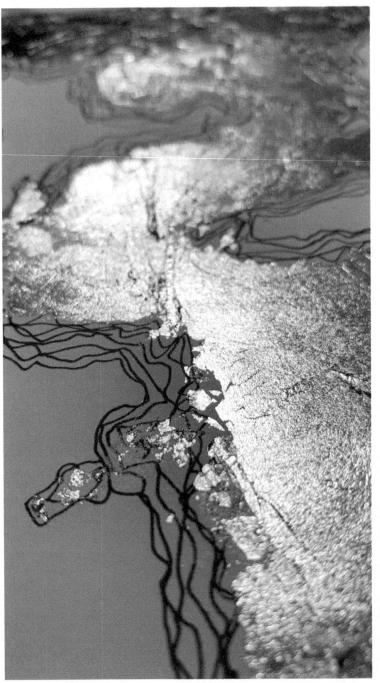

A prayer for power

Almighty, invisible God,
   we long to see your power.
We dream and sing of your triumph over
   enemies seen and unseen,
   natural and supernatural,
   foreign and domestic,
   treacherous and traitorous.
But the more I listen for your voice,
   the more I'm convinced that
we don't really know what we're asking —
   for you seem to prefer
      gentle gestures over heavy advances,
      sleight of hand over brute force,
   and whispers of truth over howls of certainty.
No, you reserve the most awe-some displays
   not to be used against enemies,
      but to reprove, rebuke, refine and
         ultimately remake us into vessels of glory.
We forget that you are the Potter
   and we are ever and always
      but clay in your hands.
Forgive our arrogance in
   trying to co-opt your power
      for earthen imaginations.
In your mercy, let us see your power anew
   and let the weight of your glory
      humble us again into submission to your will.

Amen

A prayer for listening

Lord, are you speaking?
I thought I heard you say something,
    but I'm not sure.
Sometimes the timbre of your voice
    is so easily recognizable;
other times I struggle to
    pick it out over the disquiet within
        and the din surrounding me.
Even still, I wonder if you prefer it that way,
    for even in the midst of all the babel,
        your whispers resound unrepressed,
            always finding their target —
            that is, if I'm listening.
Well, I'm listening now, Lord.
Help me to hear you better
    and to be assured that I actually heard you.
And in your mercy,
    grant me the patience
        and humility
        and willingness
        to listen.
Speak, Lord. I'm ready.

Amen

A prayer for words

Lord, sometimes I don't even know what to say.
I want to say "thank you" but the words seem inadequate.
I want to say "Yes, Lord" but the words seem hasty.
I want to say "I'm sorry" but the words seem disingenuous.
I want to say "I love you" but the words seem superficial.
I want to say so much, but the words never quite match...
    maybe I'm using too many words?
Or maybe the words aren't the problem...
Fix my heart, Lord,
    so that my words may match
        both the work you're doing in me
    and the work you intend to do through me.
And in your mercy, please let me know
    when I'm doing too much.

Amen

A prayer for light

O great Father of all the heavenly lights,
   from you emanates all things true,
      righteous and good.
In your mercy, smile upon us once more,
   that the light of your grace may bring
      clarity to our being.

O great Light of the world,
   in you all that can live lives.
In your mercy, call us by name,
   that the light of your love may summon us
      into wholeness and purpose.

O great Fire of Pentecost,
   through you is every sign and wonder
      made manifest.
In your mercy, ignite your flame within us
   so that by the light of your power
      we might boldly make plain your presence
       and salvation in the world.

Now great God — Father, Son, and Spirit —
   make us ever ready
      to face the scrutiny of your light
       as we are to live in the light.

Amen

A prayer for mercy

Lord, why is mercy so hard?
We ask and plead for mercy —
   for you to be viscerally moved
      from indifference to compassion —
but seldom do we really practice mercy.
It demands too much of us,
   the time we think we own,
   the money we think we earned,
   the pity we think we deserve,
   the image we think we must protect,
   the vulnerability we think we don't need.
Lord, we need to learn a new religion,
   where our worship is ever merciful
and mercy is always ever our sacrifice to you.
Teach us to embrace the anguish of mercy
   till our lives can make manifest its ecstasy.
In the name of Him who said:
   "Go and learn what this means,
     'I desire mercy not sacrifice.'"

Amen

A prayer for a good _____

Lord, what really makes a day good?
Is it good because the cycles of sun and moon,
   light and dark are perfectly balanced?
Is it good because nothing got screwed up,
   nothing needs fixing
     and there are no mistakes?
Is it good because there is no conflict,
   no arguments, no anger, and no rebuke?
Or is it good simply because you say so,
   you make it so?
Then what else do you say is good? Who else?
By the power of your Holy Spirit,
   give me faith to see
     the good you see
       in everything that can be seen,
and in your mercy,
   emancipate me from the prejudice
     that rejects, denies, and distorts
       the goodness you've hidden in all things.
In the name of the One who "saw all that he had made
   and it was very good."

Amen

A prayer for trusting again

Lord, I hear you say "Trust",
    and I want to say "Amen" —
but I have questions:
What does trust really look like
    and how do I know when to do nothing
        or when to take action?
Can I trust you without feeling vulnerable?
Does "love others" also mean "trust others"?
    What if I don't know how to do that?
        What if I don't want to do that?
Can I really trust You even if I don't trust them?
Can we create, nurture, and grow trust —
    even after we've lost it?
I'll wait for your answers, Lord.
In the meantime, sing over me again
    your stories of sign and symbol
        full of promises of hope
            and the dawning of new life —
    and the faithfulness of a trustworthy God.

Amen

A prayer for change

Lord, when will change —
    you know, the "little child shall lead them"
        kind of change —
    when will it finally get here?
It seems we've been waiting
    an awful long time,
and too many have grown weary,
    too many have lost hope,
    too many have suffered,
    too many have turned cruel,
    too many have given up,
    too many have died needlessly.
When, Lord? How long, Lord?
While we wait,
sing to us again your stories
    of siblings reconciled,
    of children protected from cruelty,
    of teenagers confronting giants,
    of queens stopping hatred,
    of men believing the women,
    of community communion erasing poverty,
    of violent men converted to peacemakers,
    of outsiders made family through love —
sing to us till we can see anew that
    you are still working.
And give us grace to not just wait,
    but to work with you till all the work is done.

Amen

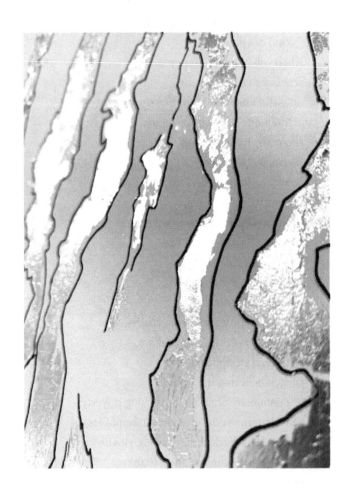

A prayer for nuance

Lord, in your abundant mercy,
   please deliver us from memes.
Deliver us from the temptation to reduce
   necessary conversations into sound bites
     and complicated relationships
     into oversimplified caricatures.
Restore to us the joy of nuance!
Save us, Lord, and remind us again
   — through trial or triumph —
of the depth and power of your loving kindness
   that risks everything to gain
     all our complexities for heaven's sake.
Teach us to do the same for each other,
   to hold in the tender tension of love
     the delicate sacred worth of every person
       till each one is loved into wholeness.
And show us daily the audacity of mercy
   as the rule of life, never the exception.
In the name of Him who said
   "Satan has asked to sift all of you as wheat.
   But I have prayed for you,
     that your faith may not fail.
   And when you have turned back,
     strengthen your brothers."

Amen

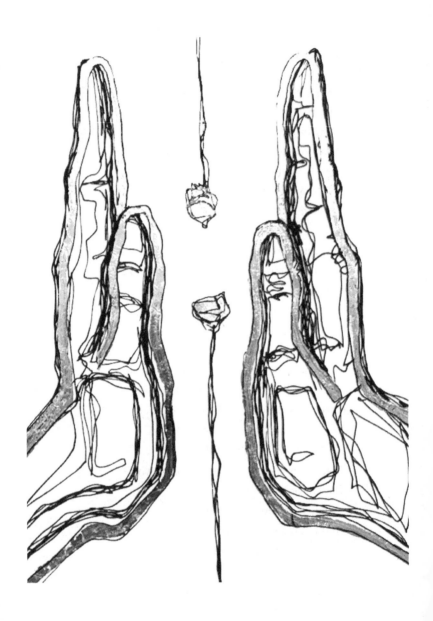

A prayer for dislike

Lord, the truth is
there are some things I just don't like —
    straight peanut butter,
    spiders and snakes,
    heavy metal music,
    clean clothes on the floor,
    overly excitable dogs,
    mayonnaise —
but apparently some of your other children do.
Lord, the truth is
there are some people I just don't like —
    the mean,
    the rude,
    the proud,
    the toxic,
    the contentious,
    the lewd —
but apparently you love them, and me, still.
Thank you for both the gift of dislike
    and for your love that supersedes it.
Work in me this power, O Lord,
so that my dislike
    may never diminish or despise or disqualify
        the stamp of your image,
        the light of your love,
    or the work of your grace within all, for all.
In the name of
    "The LORD, the LORD,
    the compassionate and gracious God,
    slow to anger,
    abounding in love and faithfulness,
    maintaining love to thousands,
    and forgiving wickedness, rebellion and sin."

Amen

A prayer for escaping violence

Lord, how can we be peacemakers
   when we cannot escape violence?
How can we know peace
   when our lives are continually disrupted by
      unfettered rage,
      unaddressed prejudice,
   and unhinged rationalization?
How can I pray for peace
   when I don't really know or trust
      that my neighbor values my life....
         or I theirs?
Breathe your peace into us again, Lord.
Speak your peace over us again, Lord.
Command your peace within us again, Lord,
   till all our hostility and hostilities
      are subverted and extinguished
         by mercy and grace.
In the name of Him who said "Peace! Be still."

Amen

A prayer for escaping death

O Merciful and Almighty God,
   you the Creator of everything that lives
      and that can live,
   you the very dawn of being itself,
shield us from the tyranny of death —
      the fear of its finality and inevitability —
   so that we can always feel in our bones
      the sustaining power of your love.

Amen

O Blessed Lord Jesus,
   you the great Redeemer of the world
      and all therein,
   you the Author and Perfecter of faith,
save us from the pathways of death —
      the temptation to create it and glorify it —
   so that we can follow you unbound and free
      by the summoning power of your love.

Amen

O Holy Ghost, Spirit of Life Divine,
   you the Comforter and Advocate
      for all those who believe,
   you the giver of peace and power,
send us to the very places of death —
      communities that have become tombs —
   so that we can be healing agents of grace
      by the resurrecting power of your love.

Amen

A prayer for traveling

Lord, I'm ready to follow you to freedom,
    but could we do it my way?
You like to travel the narrow paths
      that are filled with incredible hidden gems
    but it sometimes feels lonely.
You like to take it slow and savor each step,
    but it doesn't feel like it's making progress.
You like to stop for every pitiable person,
    but it messes up the prescribed plan.
You like to travel with very particular principles,
    but it sometimes feels outdated or obsolete.
You like to invite everybody to come along,
    but it compels generosity and friendship.
Traveling your way with you
    is sometimes awkward and difficult,
but I do like where you're going —
      I need to get to the place you are going.
So, please in your mercy,
    let me travel with you to freedom,
and give me grace to walk only and always
    in that Way that can and will lead me to life.
In the name of Him who said
    "You know the way
      to the place where I am going..."

Amen

A prayer for stopping and moving again

Lord, in you I live,
   in you I move,
      and in you I have my being,
but I think it's time to stop —
   stop complaining about the world,
      stop raging about every little thing,
   stop ignoring all the really big things,
      stop fighting just to fight,
   stop consuming just to consume,
      stop wasting time with worry,
   stop fearing the unknown,
      stop criticizing those who disagree,
   stop judging those in need,
      stop. Stop. STOP!
As I rest here in your presence,
   teach me, Lord Jesus,
      how to move again
   to the cadence of sacrifice and mercy,
      of grace and love.

Amen

A prayer for exodus

O God of endless mercy,
you greet us in each moment,
    offering a revival of hope for renewed living
    in your kingdom —
but we are creatures interrupted by fear,
    enticed into believing both that
        life is controlled by fear
and that fear is the means to control life.
We need exodus, Lord!
By the power of your Spirit
release us into the freedom of expectancy
    so that we might learn again how to see
        the miraculous potential of each moment
            and to trust again that your mercy
            outruns every moment.
And for love's sake,
    lead us to the place of
    humble, compassionate courage,
where honesty, integrity and kindness
    can overrule a culture of mistrust, suspicion,
    and pretentious strength,
so that we may have a right mind
    to more fully know the true power of love.
In the name of the One who continues to say:
    "Take courage! It is I. Do not be afraid."

Amen

A prayer for better

Lord, I need a new attitude.
I need a better way to cope —
   cause I get too easily overwhelmed.
I need a better way to listen —
   cause I can't make sense of it anymore.
I need a better way to care —
   cause I can't be this angry all the time.
I need a better way to give —
   cause I don't know how to help.
I need a better way to fight —
   cause I can't do it alone.
I need a better way to stand up —
   cause I can't be silent anymore.
I need a better way to be and become
   a child of your choosing,
   a citizen of your kingdom.
So, fix me, dear Lord.
Teach me how to get rid of
   the inertia of my malaise
and help me to embrace
   the ease of your good cheer
     and the clarity of your summons —
til all my ways of living and being
   are subverted into purposed newness.
In the name of Him who said
   "I came that they may have life,
     and have it more abundantly."

Amen

A prayer for returning

Lord, I don't know how to "come home."
I know I'm not supposed to be in this place
but I can't seem to leave my dis-ease.
I know I am anointed with sacred potential,
but I can't seem to shake my doubt.
I know I'm supposed to lead by example,
but I can't seem to abandon my sin.
Lord, I don't know how to "come home,"
but I'm trying.
Please work your power in me to know again
that leaving is possible only because
you've brought home to me.

Amen

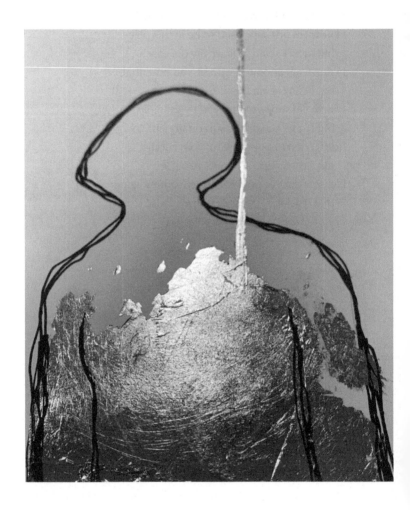

A prayer for love

O Lord of life,
if you are love and love is patient and kind —
    then aren't you tired?
Don't we just wear you out sometimes?
I get too exhausted trying to love your people.
I get too exhausted trying to love myself.
But I guess that's the point
    you so lovingly keep trying to teach me:
stop trying so hard to manufacture love,
    just be loved then you can become loving.
Is it really that simple, Lord?
Then sing over and through me again
a love that is
    relentless in its pursuit,
    fierce in its care,
    boundless in its embrace,
    unfathomable in its particularity, and
undaunted by rejection, betrayal, or malice —
till all my weariness is exhausted
    and I am made whole and new again.
In the name of Jesus who
    "having loved his own who were in the world,
        he loved them fully, to the very end."

Amen

A prayer for the journey

How far is it, Lord?
How far exactly is this path we're on
   and where does it all lead?
I thought we were just heading home but
you keeping stopping —
   for resting and praying,
   for healing and raising,
   for comforting and confronting,
   for encouraging and sending,
   for weeping and suffering,
   for dying and living again.
Your stops are never convenient
   and rarely make sense,
   yet always timely, relevant, and essential.
Teach me this grace, O Lord.
How far is it, Lord?
Do we have time for another stop?

Amen

PART 3
Promise

Today is the day

Today is the day, Lord.
If the heavens can stretch its arms
   wide enough to hold all the worlds you have made,
      then so can I — today is the day.
If the sun can bring warmth and beauty
   to both the meadow and the trash heap,
      then so can I — today is the day.
If the leaves can so easily change and
   find their purpose with each season,
      then so can I — today is the day.
If the birds can never grow weary of
   singing their songs even in the cold of winter,
      then so can I — today is the day.
If the ants can never stop building and
   fighting for the common good,
      then so can I — today is the day.
If the groundhog can periodically stop
   to rest deeply in your provision and protection,
      then so can I — today is the day.
If the infant can still so easily delight in others
   who may or may not have their best interests in mind,
      then so can I — today is the day.
Today is the day, Lord,
   for me to be renewed and re-created by your grace,
till the splendor of your image is made clear
   in my being,
      my doing,
         my speaking,
            my waiting,
               my resting.

Amen

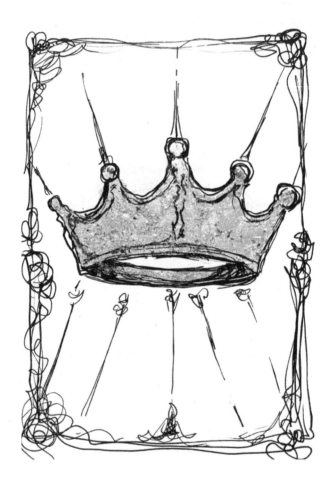

To God, the Lord

O God in heaven,
help me to remember that
   you are Lord of everything —
      be it beautiful or obscene, you are Lord;
      be it frightening or enlivening, you are Lord;
      be it peaceful or chaotic, you are Lord —
   and nothing can change that,
      not my worship nor my doubt,
      not my sin nor my holiness,
      not my prayers nor my silence.

Yet, I confess that too often
   I squander my trust,
      listening more to pundits and doom scrolling
        than simply being still in your presence.

Forgive me, Lord.
Teach me again
   how to rest in your lordship, confident that
      your rule and work remains as always
        undeterred by me.

Amen

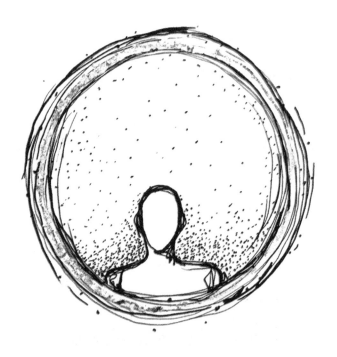

To the God of Every Time

O great God of all there ever was —
  please fix my memory.
Remind me again that the season changed,
  that night ended,
and that though it was hard
  letting go was ultimately good for me.
Help me to see the past
  not as a record of my drama
    but a testimony of your faithfulness.

O great God of all that is —
  please protect my mind and heart.
Shield me from every thing that would destroy,
  every thing that masquerades as truth,
  every thing that depletes hope —
    whether from another or self-inflicted,
Keep me and guard me with peace
  till my life and my world become peaceable.

O great God of all that is to come —
  please empower my dreaming.
Spark a new hope within me
  to know deeply that all things are possible
    and nothing is ever lost.
Teach me to sing a new song,
  to write a new melody,
    to dance a new dance.
Show me just how endless joy can be.

Amen. Amen. Amen.

To a Generous God

Most gracious and generous Lord,
thank you for a place in your kingdom,
   for sins forgiven and a heart set free,
   for assurance of life eternal and
      an eternal life of assurance —
   but please forgive me for asking:
Are you serious? Was all this just for me?
If I've got a place in your kingdom,
   can I get one for my cousin, too?
If I've got forgiveness,
   can my neighbor get it, too?
If I've got freedom,
   can my coworker be free, too?
If I've got assurance,
   can my children have it, too?
Lord, if you will give so generously to these
   all the same blessings as me,
then why is it so hard to believe
   that my enemies can have it all, too?
In your mercy,
teach me how to be
   an open-handed Giver like you,
so that I may have the grace to advocate
   as fiercely for the stranger
      as I do for the friend.

Amen

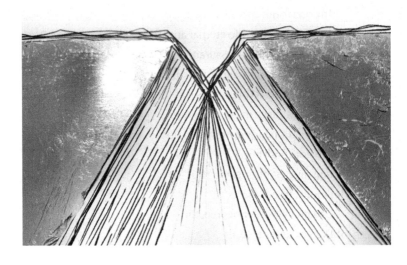

To the God of the In-Between

Lord, I'm grateful for how you so lovingly and graciously
    preside over all my beginnings and endings,
        assuring and reassuring me time and time again
        that you hold both firmly in your hands.
But I'm wondering still about the in-between —
    the place where I seem to dwell more often than not,
        too far from the start to remember your promises,
        too far from the end to envision your glory.

In the uncertainty of this in-betweenness
    I am bankrupted by a vacancy of purpose
        and sabotaged by the intrusion of fear.
So, I need you to be God
    of not just of my beginning and end
        but of my in-between,
and tell me again the stories of cloud and pillar,
    of manna and water,
    of ravens and angels,
    of rod and staff
        and goodness and mercy —
till I can see my in-between not as purposeless penalty
    but as intentional preparation for newness.
In the name of the One who said "Remember the long way..."

Amen

To the God of Communion and Community

O God of communion and community,
I'm grateful for a place at your table
  where even my deepest hunger
    is overmatched and satisfied
      by your provision.

Thank you for my place.
I'm grateful for a seat at your table
  where I am lovingly known
and the singularity of my personage
  is gracefully woven into the tapestry
    of your family.

Thank you for my seat.
Now, Lord, as I come to my own table,
  show me how even what I have
    can yet become daily bread for those
      still searching for their place.

And in your mercy,
teach me better table manners
  so that I may never take my seat
    without also helping another find theirs.

Amen

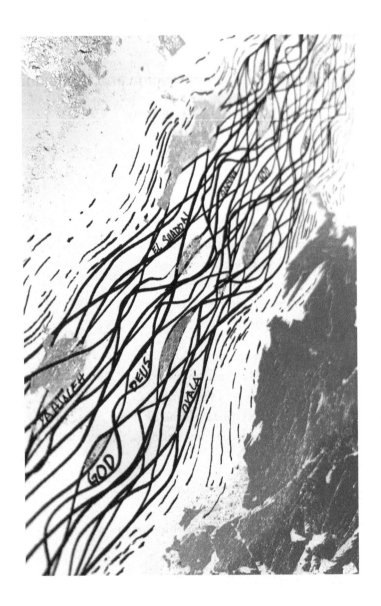

In the Name Of

O most holy and gracious God,
It is your name we reverence
   in mellifluous praise and dutiful obeisance,
it is your name we invoke
   for righteous justice and just mercy;
It is your name we confront
   in awed investigation and interrogation —
but do we really know who you are?
Do we really know Your Name
   or do we only know who we wish you to be?
Speak to us your sacred name
   and tell us again who you are
   so that our lives and our living
      may be re-tuned to praise you more perfectly.

Amen

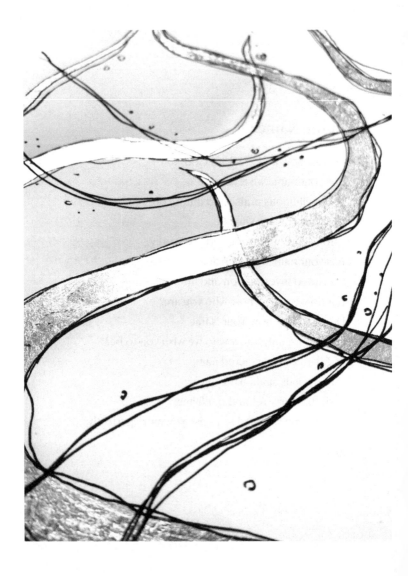

To the God Who Weeps

Merciful God,
please stay and weep with us a while.
Weep with us for neighbors
   who struggle to live free and
      yearn for freedom to live.
Weep with us for children
   whose dreams are continuously hijacked
      by sacred trust squandered.
Weep with us for families
   who cannot escape the abuse of poverty
      nor the poverty of abuse.
Weep with us for those
   who daily carry the wounds
      of excommunication and exile.
Weep with us for the many who feel
   that their lives hold more value
      in death than life.
Weep with us for those
   who cope by trampling over dignity
      and delighting in suffering.
Weep with us for us
   who love to claim rightness
      but resist every truthful correction.
Weep with us, Lord.
Stay with us awhile...
   and when we are ready,
      call us forth into resurrection.

Amen

To a Gracious God

O Lord God, Sovereign Almighty,
you are ruler of the heavens and the earth
    and all the depths imaginable —
even still, I wonder sometimes
    why do you bother with us?
It would seem to me that you may have
    more important things to do than to
        listen to our grumblings,
        tend to our petitions,
        arbitrate our squabbles,
        resolve our doubts,
        redeem our mistakes,
        ennoble our self-worth,
    and resurrect our frail lives.
Yet, here we are —
confronted again by
    the peculiar particularity of your love for us
        and the extravagance of your grace
            ever toward us and working for us.
Please, Lord, in your mercy,
keep the wonder of grace ever before me
    that I may continuously marvel at its beauty
        and by it become more graceful,
            grace-filled and
                gracious.

Amen

To a "Do Nothing" God

Lord, I just don't like it when you say "be still."
Please don't ask me anymore.
I want to move and know that I'm moving.
I want to act and know the purpose of action.
I want to do something and
   know that something is being done —
but you keep saying "be still."
   Be still.
      BE.
         STILL.

Teach me how to delight in
   the stillness of grace
till all my doing is undone and
   my knowing becomes perfected praise.

Amen

To the Compassionate God

O God,
I confess that sometimes I just don't care.
Yes, I can see the tears,
    I can hear the pleas,
    I can recognize the hunger,
    I can sense the humiliation,
    I can feel the desperation
      mixed with suspicion,
    I can acknowledge the grind and the hustle,
yet I struggle to actually care,
    to feel the pangs of compassion for others,
    to actually be moved by their plight
      and affected by their stories...
        and I am ashamed.
I should, but I don't — and I don't know why.
Forgive me, and please set me free.
Forgive me, please. Set me free.
Teach me the beauty and power of
    a compassion that isn't pious nor piteous
      but embodies "God with us."
And in your mercy,
    enlarge the boundaries of heart —
      even if it must hurt to care.
In the name of "The LORD! The LORD!
    a God who is compassionate and merciful,
      very patient,
        full of great loyalty and faithfulness."

Amen

To the God of Yes/No

O God of steadfast love and boundless mercy,
you overwhelm and overmatch our lives
   with goodness beyond measure,
day after day affirming and confirming
   your promises of blessing.
Thank you, Lord, for the strength of your "Yes,"
  but now, please,
     teach us the power of your "No."
Teach us the "No" of a potter
  who so skillfully perfects the clay
    into a purposed vessel of beauty.
Show us the "No" of a shepherd
  who so dutifully hems in the flock
    from both straying and strays.
Speak to us the "No" of a friend
  who so lovingly invites companions
    to know and become their truest selves.
O God, by your Spirit, work in us this power
  so that we may be unafraid
    of your holy disruptions,
  and gladly welcome your "No,"
    not as punishment,
      but as merely a variation on the theme:
"Yes and Amen."

Scripture References

Praise for mirrors and windows
John 1:39 NRSV "He said to them, 'Come and see.' They came and saw where he was staying, and they remained with him that day. It was about four o'clock in the afternoon."

For a more perfect praise
Matthew 6:9 NIV "This, then, is how you should pray: 'Our Father in heaven, hallowed be your name...'"

A prayer for the caring
Psalm 145:8 NIV "The LORD is gracious and compassionate, slow to anger and rich in love."

A prayer for the still mad
John 3:17 NIV "For God did not send his Son into the world to condemn the world, but to save the world through him."

A prayer for healing
Exodus 15:26 CEB "The LORD said, 'If you are careful to obey the LORD your God, do what God thinks is right, pay attention to his commandments, and keep all of his regulations, then I won't bring on you any of the diseases that I brought on the Egyptians. I am the LORD who heals you.'"

A prayer for all peoples
John 17:21–22 NIV "...that all of them may be one, Father, just as you are in me and I am in you. May they also be in us so that the world may believe that you have sent me. I have given them the glory that you gave me, that they may be one as we are one—I in them and you in me—so that they may be brought to complete unity. Then the world will know that you sent me and have loved them even as you have loved me."

A prayer for truth
Genesis 3:9 NIV "But the LORD God called to the man, 'Where are you?'"

Genesis 3:11 NIV "And he said, 'Who told you that you were naked? Have you eaten from the tree that I commanded you not to eat from?'"

Genesis 18:14 NIV "'Is anything too hard for the LORD? I will return to you at the appointed time next year, and Sarah will have a son.'"

1 Samuel 16:1 NRSV "The LORD said to Samuel, 'How long will you grieve over Saul? I have rejected him from being king over Israel. Fill your horn with oil and set out; I will send you to Jesse the Bethlehemite, for I have provided for myself a king among his sons.'"

Isaiah 6:8 NRSV "Then I heard the voice of the LORD saying, 'Whom shall I send, and who will go for us?' And I said, 'Here am I; send me!'"

Malachi 3:8 NRSV "Will anyone rob God? Yet you are robbing me! But you say, 'How are we robbing you?' In your tithes and offerings!"

A prayer for innocence
Luke 18:16 ESV "But Jesus called them to him, saying, 'Let the children come to me, and do not hinder them, for to such belongs the kingdom of God.'" *See also Matthew 19:14 and Mark 10:14*

A prayer for mercy
Matthew 9:13 NIV "But go and learn what this means: 'I desire mercy, not sacrifice.' For I have not come to call the righteous, but sinners."

A prayer for a good _____
Genesis 1:31a NIV "God saw all that he had made, and it was very good."

A prayer for change
Isaiah 11:6 NIV "The wolf will live with the lamb, the leopard will lie down with the goat, the calf and the lion and the yearling together; and a little child will lead them."

A prayer for nuance
Luke 22:31b–32 NIV "Satan has asked to sift all of you as wheat. But I have prayed for you, that your faith may not fail. And when you have turned back, strengthen your brothers."

A prayer for dislike
Exodus 34:6–7a NIV "And he passed in front of Moses, proclaiming, 'The LORD, the LORD, the compassionate and gracious God, slow to anger, abounding in love and faithfulness, maintaining love to thousands, and forgiving wickedness, rebellion and sin.'"

A prayer for escaping violence
Mark 4:39 NRSV "He woke up and rebuked the wind, and said to the sea, 'Peace! Be still!' Then the wind ceased, and there was a dead calm."

A prayer for traveling
John 14:1–4 NIV "Do not let your hearts be troubled. You believe in God; believe also in me. My Father's house has many rooms; if that were not so, would I have told you that I am going there to prepare a place for you? And if I go and prepare a place for you, I will come back and take you to be with me that you also may be where I am. You know the way to the place where I am going."

A prayer for exodus
Matthew 14:26–27 NIV "When the disciples saw him walking on the lake, they were terrified. 'It's a ghost,' they said, and cried out in fear. But Jesus immediately said to them: 'Take courage! It is I. Don't be afraid.'"

A prayer for better
John 10:10 NRSV "The thief comes only to steal and kill and destroy. I came that they may have life, and have it abundantly."

A prayer for love
John 13:1 NRSV "Now before the festival of the Passover, Jesus knew that his hour had come to depart from this world and go to the Father. Having loved his own who were in the world, he loved them to the end."

To the God of the In-Between
Deuteronomy 8:2 NRSV "Remember the long way that the LORD your God has led you these forty years in the wilderness, in order to humble you, testing you to know what was in your heart, whether or not you would keep his commandments."

To a "Do Nothing" God
Psalm 46:10 NRSV "Be still, and know that I am God! I am exalted among the nations; I am exalted in the earth."

To the Compassionate God
Exodus 34:6 CEB "The LORD passed in front of him and proclaimed: "The LORD! The LORD! a God who is compassionate and merciful, very patient, full of great loyalty and faithfulness."

To the God of Yes/No
2 Corinthians 1:20 NKJV "For all the promises of God in Him are Yes, and in Him Amen, to the glory of God through us."

Artist's Notes

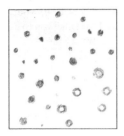

Praise for wonders
I like to imagine a space where all the wonders just appear here and there like golden stars floating, coming to us.

Praise for mirror and windows
This shows two individual faces in two mirrors that become one frame. Jesus asked us to look at others as we look at ourselves.

Praise for grace
In Brazil we say: *God's graces arrive in winding paths.*

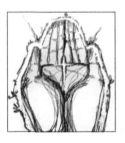

A prayer for healing
If God needs to give us His only Son to save and heal the world, I'm sure He will do it as many times as we need.

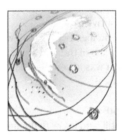

A prayer for remembering
Here I have that unknown form, almost like a cell, like a formation of memory, a vague space in our mind that brings golden memories.

A prayer for mercy
God is perfect as a complete circle, but we are not. We cannot be as complete as God in doing mercy, but we want to be, we strive to be.

A prayer for stopping and moving again
We are in God's energy, stopping and going in pulses.

A prayer for exodus
The path that Moses opens on the sea to a new beginning, the golden path surrounded by chaos.

A prayer for love
One of the most amazing things about God is that He never gives up on us. We can be totally empty but He will keep filling with His love. It's like a line of water on our hearts that never stops, every day filling us. But we never get full because we are human and we are broken. We can't just fully trust.

To a Generous God
A golden heart. Royal, powerful and generous as God's heart. Different from the man, that is simple and weak.

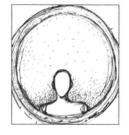

To the God of Every Time
How big and how full God is! We have the opportunity to be part of all that and at the same time be part of Him. A God who is there all the time and gave us everything.

Made in the USA
Las Vegas, NV
14 November 2023